OUTSIDE AND INSIDE
SPIDERS

BY SANDRA MARKLE

SCHOLASTIC INC.
New York Toronto London Auckland Sydney
Mexico City New Delhi Hong Kong

*For Mary Larson, librarian at
the Fernbank Science Center, Atlanta, Georgia,
with thanks for all you do. Your friendliness makes
thc Fcrnbank Library a warm, wonderful place to do research.*

*The author would especially like to thank Dr. Petra Sierwald,
research associate for the Field Museum of Natural History,
Chicago, Illinois, for sharing her expertise and enthusiasm.*

ISBN 0-439-17314-0

Copyright © 1994 by Sandra Markle. All rights reserved.
Published by Scholastic Inc., 555 Broadway, New York, NY 10012,
by arrangement with Aladdin Paperbacks, an imprint of Simon &
Schuster Children's Publishing Division. SCHOLASTIC and
associated logos are trademarks and/or registered trademarks of
Scholastic Inc.

12 11 10 9 8 7 6 5 4 3 2   0 1 2 3 4 5/0

Printed in the U.S.A.   08

First Scholastic printing, February 2000

The text of this book was set in 15 point Melior.
Designed by Joseph Rutt

*Note to parents and teachers: To help young readers pronounce
words that are likely to be unfamiliar, a pronunciation guide is
presented on page 35. The first appearance of these words is
italicized. For children who might like to know exactly how many
times the magnified images have been enlarged, this information
can be found with the photo credits on page 39. The symbol **x** after
the number means "times."*

*Don't worry,
this tarantula is used to
being handled. Tarantulas
are the biggest spiders.
Some have leg spans
nearly ten inches
across and weigh about
as much as half a stick
of margarine.*

Like you, spiders are special living things. You may not have seen one as big as this *tarantula*, but you are sure to have seen a smaller one. Spiders can be found walking across the ground or climbing up a wall. They can even be spotted dangling from the ceiling on a silk thread. So how does a spider live? What's inside, and how does its body work? This book will let you take a close look and even peek inside a spider to find out.

FISHING SPIDER

PEDIPALPS

SOLDIER BEETLE

ANTENNAE

See the slim antennae sticking out of the soldier beetle's head? Insects have antennae to help them be aware of what is going on around them. Spiders never have antennae. But look at the fishing spider's head. What look like short legs just below its eyes are called pedipalps. Spiders have pedipalps close to their mouths to help them catch and hold onto food. Insects do not have pedipalps.

First, you need to know how to tell a spider from an insect. They often look similar at first glance, but they are not really alike.

Look closely at the fishing spider and the soldier beetle. One quick way to tell the difference is that spiders have eight legs. Insects like the soldier beetle have only six legs. Spiders also never have wings. Many insects do.

A spider's body has two main parts. Do you see them? The head and chest are joined into one big part which connects to the *abdomen* by a slim waist. An insect's body usually has a separate head, chest, and abdomen.

This is a comb-footed spider. It is drawing out a silk strand with its leg. You have probably seen this spider's silk webs. Comb-footed spiders make themselves at home in people's houses. Their webs are often called cobwebs.

All spiders also make silk, and they do it their entire lives. Some insects make silk, but only during one phase of their lives.

A spider's silk is made as a liquid in special body parts called silk glands. The silk flows through tubes and out tiny *spigots* on the spider's tail end. To form strands, the spider fastens its silk to something, like a leaf, and then walks away. Or it may attach the silk to a leg and pull. No one is quite sure why, but pulling on the liquid silk makes it change to a solid strand.

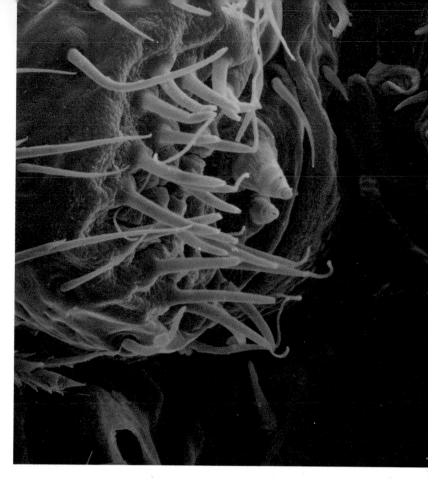

magnified and color-enhanced

This picture is a very close look at a black widow spider's tail end. See what looks like tubes and cones? These are spigots where the silk shoots out. Spiders can make different kinds of silk, such as sticky silk and strong cable-like lines. The different-shaped spigots are connected to different types of silk glands to make different kinds of silk. The spider can also make thicker silk strands by releasing silk from several spigots at the same time.

Spiders use their silk in a lot of different ways. Some spiders spin silk webs to trap food. Different types of spiders spin different types of webs. There are webs that look like a tangle of threads, and others that are funnel shaped. The most familiar is the orb-shaped web like this one built by a garden spider.

To build its web, the spider first spins a silk frame. Next, it adds strands like spokes on a bicycle wheel. Then, going from the hub out, it spins a temporary spiral of widely spaced threads crossing over the spokes. Finally, as it moves back to the hub, the spider removes the temporary spiral and spins a spiral with strands placed close together. To make the web a really good trap, this new spiral is coated with sticky drops.

See the glue droplets on the threads that caught this midge? Silk is amazingly strong and stretchy, but insects may still break free. Wind and rain also damage webs. The spider usually repairs or rebuilds its web every day. To save energy, the spider recycles, eating the old web threads before making new silk.

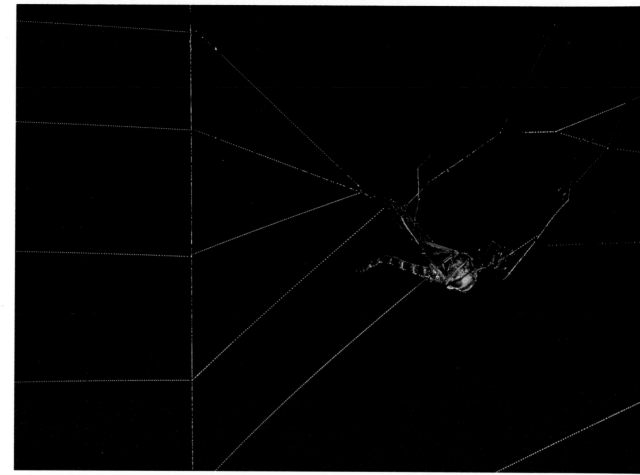

Some spiders that build web traps stay on the web's hub, waiting to pounce. Others use their silk to make a signal thread. They connect this to their web. Then they hide out of sight, holding onto the thread. A jerk on the thread signals a catch. The spider plucks its web threads to judge where the insect is stuck. Then it rushes along an unsticky spoke thread to make the kill.

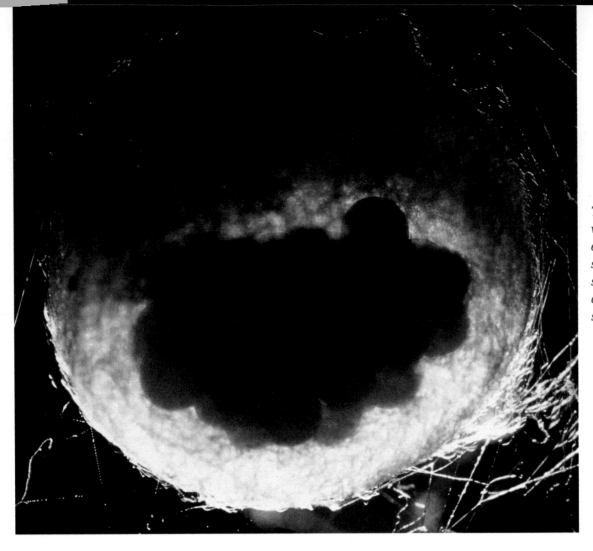

This black widow's egg sac is really very small—only about as big as the end of your little finger. It has been lit so you can peek through the silk to see the eggs inside. Silk strands around the outside connect the egg sac to the mother's web.

Another way spiders use silk is to protect their eggs. Some spiders spin no more than a thin silk blanket. Most, though, make an egg sac by building up layer upon layer of silk around their eggs. This sac protects the eggs from heat and cold, rain and sun.

Some spiders also use their silk to build nests. Orb-web weavers use their silk-like twine to roll up a leaf. Then they hide inside this shelter. Funnel-web spiders spin a silk tube that connects to their web. Wolf spiders use their jaws to dig a tunnel in the ground and line it with silk.

Spiders depend on their silk to keep them safe. As a spider moves from place to place, it spins out a silk thread. And every once in a while, it stops to glue down this line. It does this by pressing its tail end to the surface several times. This makes a disk of looped silk threads which anchor the line.

A spider's silk safety line keeps it from getting hurt if it suddenly steps off something high up. It also lets the spider drop to make a quick escape from an enemy.

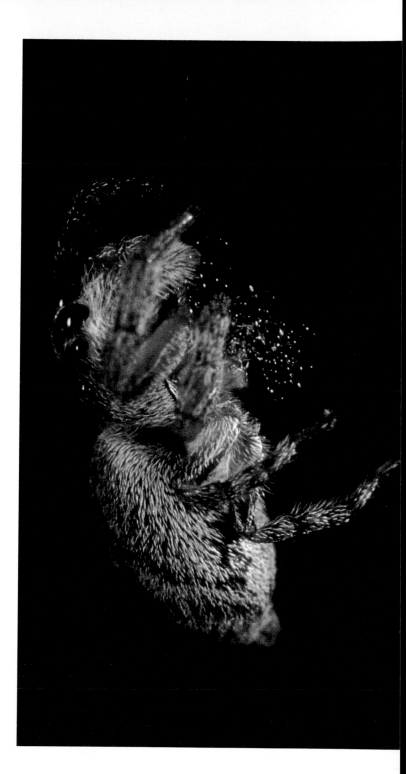

This spider dropped down by spinning out a silk line. Now it is climbing back up. See the shiny silk the spider is gathering up as it climbs? The spider will eat the silk it collects before spinning more.

*This is a trap-door spider. It is lifting the silk door it spun for its
tunnel nest. To catch food, this spider hides inside its tunnel.
When an insect or another spider comes close, the spider pushes
up its door and jumps out.*

Here's another way a spider stays safe. The covering of its body is
made of a stiff, tough material similar to your fingernails. The spider
can only bend its body at joints. These are softer parts where two stiff
parts meet. The lighter bands on this trap-door spider's legs are joints.

This tough body suit also gives the spider its shape. A spider's body
does not have a framework of bones inside the way your body does.
Except for a few places where its stiff armor projects inside, the spider's body is completely soft.

Look closely. What looks like two spiders at first glance is really one spider next to the body suit it just shed. Crawling out of an old body suit is called *molting*.

Imagine a spider growing bigger inside its stiff armor. When the spider's body becomes too big to fit, the body suit splits open. But this is not the end of the spider. By the time the old suit is outgrown, a new body suit has already formed.

Once the spider has shed its old suit, the new suit starts to harden. It may take as long as several hours for the suit to become completely hard. So to stay safe, the spider usually hides during this time. It also keeps bending its legs to help the joints stay stretchy.

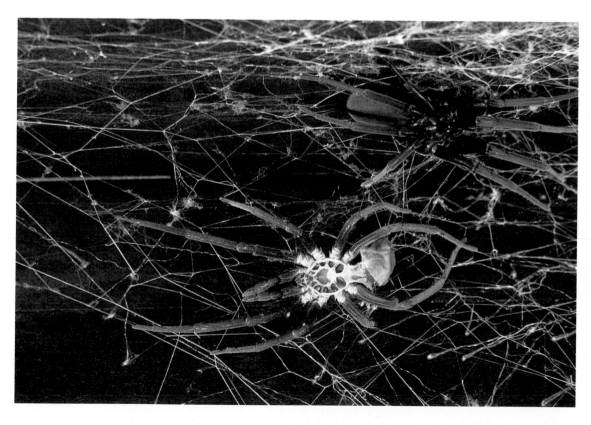

See the holes where the spider pulled its legs out of its old body suit? Before the old suit split open, most of the material that made it hard was taken back into the spider's body. This let those materials be used again and weakened the old suit. Special juices also poured out, helping to separate the old suit from the new one underneath it.

Do you see the thin line that is holding the spider safely on the flower? The little black spots above the spider's yellow fangs and pedipalps are its eyes.

To grow bigger and be active, a spider needs to eat. All spiders are hunters, and what they catch to eat is called their *prey*. Most spiders eat insects and other spiders. Some eat small fish. A few of the biggest tarantulas eat small birds and mice.

Spiders have strong mouth parts they can use to grasp and pinch. Most also have *venom*, a liquid poison. When the spider bites, a little venom flows through a tube inside the fang and out a hole just behind the tip. The venom may kill. Or it may only make the prey unable to move.

Some spiders use tricks to catch their prey. The yellow crab spider sitting very still on a yellow flower was hard to spot. When the bee got close enough, the spider sprang and sank in its fangs.

The white sac is where the spider's venom is made and stored. Normally, the fang rests tucked into a groove, but it moves out when the spider bites. Some spiders have small teeth on the edges of this groove.

15

Some spiders go looking for food. When the jumping spider spotted its insect prey, it slowly crept closer. Then it pounced, grabbing the insect with its front legs and sinking in its fangs.

When you jump, muscles pull on your bones to stretch out your legs. Spiders have muscles too, but they can only pull the spider's legs toward its body. To stretch them out, the spider's special body fluids rush into its legs. Did you ever pour water into a balloon and see it expand? The jumping spider's legs stretch the same way. But it happens very fast, launching the spider into the air.

A jumping spider can leap over twenty-five times its own body length. Imagine how far you would go if you could leap twenty-five times your body's length!

See the silk safety line trailing out behind this spider? Besides catching food, jumping spiders leap to get away from enemies and to get from one side of a hole to the other.

Some spiders that live in dark caves don't have any eyes. But most spiders have eight. Even with so many eyes, most spiders do not see well. A spider's small eyes can usually only tell if something is moving or still. Only spiders that go hunting for food, like jumping spiders and this wolf spider, have big eyes that can see details.

Spiders that hunt at night often have a special layer at the back of their big eyes. It acts like a mirror to bounce light back into the eye. On a dark night, this reflected light makes the spider's eyes seem to glow.

See how this jumping spider's hairs are set in sockets? As each hair moves, it sends messages about its position to the spider's brain. Then the brain uses this information to signal the spider's response.

magnified and color-enhanced

This is the tip of a jumping spider's foot. Some spiders, like this jumping spider, also have a tuft of hair at the tip of each foot. Although no one knows for sure just how it works, this tuft lets spiders walk straight up walls and across ceilings. Do you see the claw that also helps this spider hang on?

magnified and color-enhanced

claw

For most spiders, the most important sense is touch. And they feel with the many hairs covering their bodies and legs. Special long, thin hairs sense the slightest air movement. Even a fly's wingbeats are enough to let the spider know where to strike to catch the fly.

Besides touch, a spider's hairs have other uses. Tarantulas have hairs with sharp barbs. A tarantula rubs a leg against its body to fire these hairs at an enemy. Most spiders have special hairs on their pedipalps and feet. These let the spider taste what they touch. Imagine what it would be like to taste what you stepped on!

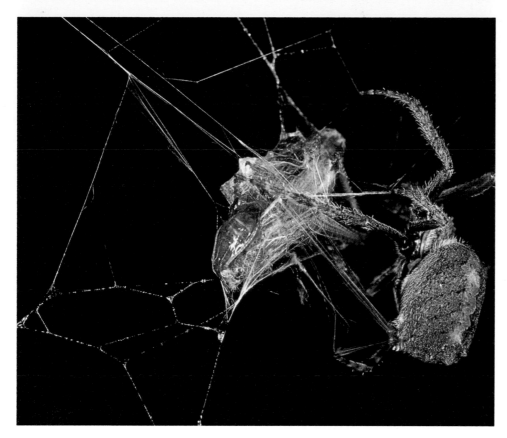

Sometimes more than one prey is trapped on the web at one time. Then the spider will eat one right away and leave the other wrapped up for later. Spiders are rarely so lucky, though. They often go weeks and even months between meals.

This large orb-web weaver felt its web move the instant the cricket landed. Then the spider rushed to attack. It turned the cricket around and around with its feet while shooting out silk. Wrapped up, the cricket could not escape or bite the spider. Next, the large orb-web weaver sank its fangs through the silk to inject its venom.

Before settling down to eat, the spider tugged the cricket to the web's hub and attached it with a silk line. The large orb-web weaver is less likely to be spotted by an enemy at the hub.

Tiny claws on this large orb-web weaver's feet let it run quickly along its web threads without falling off.

21

Spiders have very small mouths. And just like spiders, insects have a hard body suit. So to eat, the large orb-web weaver first broke open this armor with its strong-toothed jaws. Next, it threw up special juices from its stomach onto the cricket's soft inner body.

Within a few seconds, whatever the juices touched turned to a liquid. The spider sucked in this liquid. Then it threw up more of the juices and sucked in more food. At the end of the meal, nothing was left but pieces of the cricket's hard body suit.

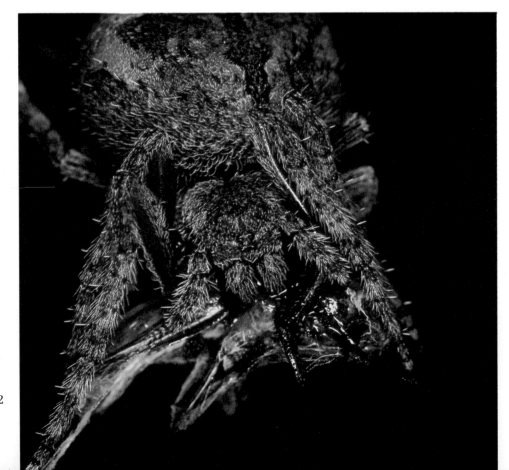

See the shiny drop of liquid between the spider's hairy jaws? That is a drop of liquid food that the spider is sucking in.

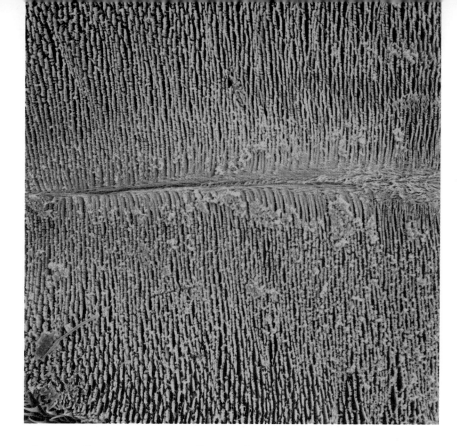

As a spider sucks in, its food flows through a screen-like plate. You can see why only liquid food will pass through the tiny holes. Anything bigger is caught. Then the spider throws up, getting rid of these hard scraps.

magnified and color-enhanced

The spider's liquid food passes through its stomach and into a special body part where it is broken down further. Then the food moves into long tubes that branch throughout the spider's body—even into its legs. This food is made up of *nutrients*, such as protein and vitamins, which pass through the tube walls and enter the spider's blood. The blood carries the nutrients to all parts of the spider's body.

As the blood flows through the spider's body, it also picks up wastes. These are produced when the spider is active. Along the way, the blood passes through special tubes that have a brush-like lining. There the wastes are strained out. They pass into a storage sac, where they pack together. Finally, the wastes are dumped out of the body through an opening at the spider's tail end.

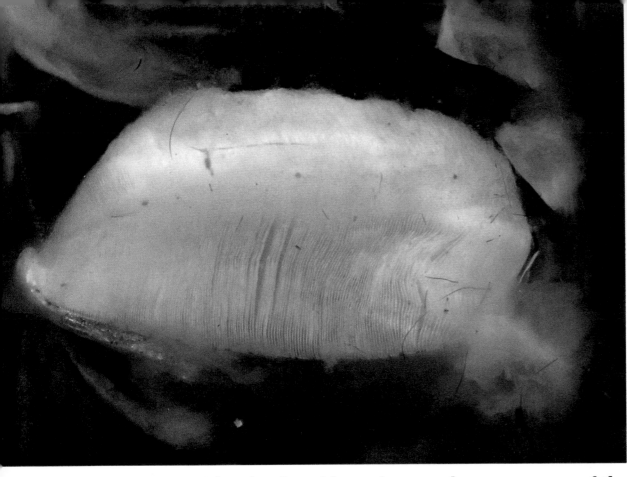

This is one of a tarantula's lungs. A tarantula has four lungs; most spiders only have two. Because a spider's lungs are made up of stacks of paper-thin blood-filled layers, they are called book lungs. In between each layer, there is an air-filled pocket. In addition to lungs, some spiders also have special tubes that carry air. The air enters these tubes through holes in the spider's abdomen. Some very tiny spiders have only these air tubes.

Besides food, spiders also need *oxygen*, one of the gases in air, to be active. But a spider does not breathe in and out through a nose and mouth the way you do. Instead, air just seeps into its lungs through slits in its abdomen. Once air is inside the lungs, oxygen moves into the blood. Then the blood carries the oxygen to all parts of the spider's body.

The spider's body uses the oxygen and food nutrients to produce the energy needed to live and grow. And it gives off a waste gas called *carbon dioxide*. This enters the blood and is carried back to the lungs. There the carbon dioxide seeps out of the slits in the spider's abdomen.

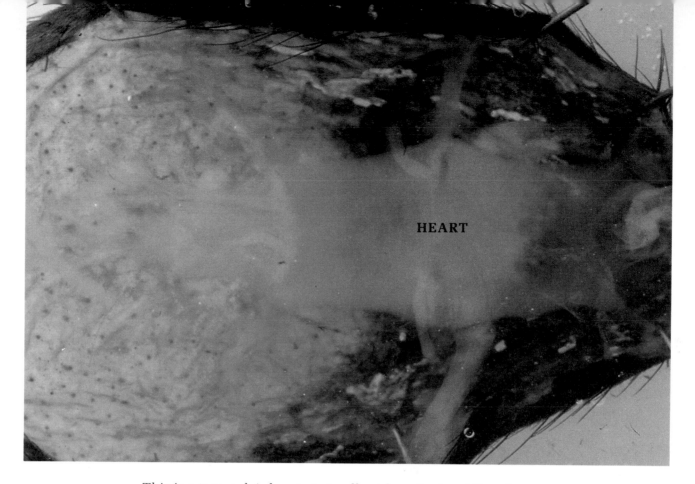

HEART

This is a tarantula's heart. As in all spiders, the heart lies along the upper back of the abdomen. The smaller tubes you can see have been cut. They are really much longer—long enough to reach even to the tips of the spider's legs.

You have been reading about blood moving around a spider's body. The pump that pushes the blood is the heart. It is a tube-shaped muscle.

When the heart squeezes, the blood inside is pushed into smaller tubes. These carry the blood to all parts of the spider's body. When the tubes end, the blood flows out, flooding the spider's body parts. Then it slowly seeps back to the heart.

These two male jumping spiders are fighting for a mate.

Perhaps the most important part of a spider's life is having young. When spiders are ready to mate, the male spiders go searching for females of their own kind.

Some spiders do special things to attract a mate. One type of male nursery spider carries along a wrapped fly as a gift. Some kinds of jumping spiders, like the ones in the picture, fight for a mate. Other male jumping spiders do a zigzagging dance to win a female's favor.

Does it surprise you to learn that these are both red-back spiders? The bigger one is the female. The smaller one is the male. Female spiders are usually bigger and stronger than male spiders. So when a male red-back spider comes courting, he makes sure the female knows he isn't food. To signal her, he shakes his abdomen and taps her web with his pedipalps and front legs.

See what looks like two shiny balls near the male's mouth? These are his pedipalps swollen to carry sperm. When the male places his sperm into an opening on the female's abdomen, they will join with her eggs. Once an egg and sperm unite, a baby spider will begin to develop.

These are red-back spiders, commonly found in Australia and New Zealand. They are closely related to black widow spiders found in the United States.

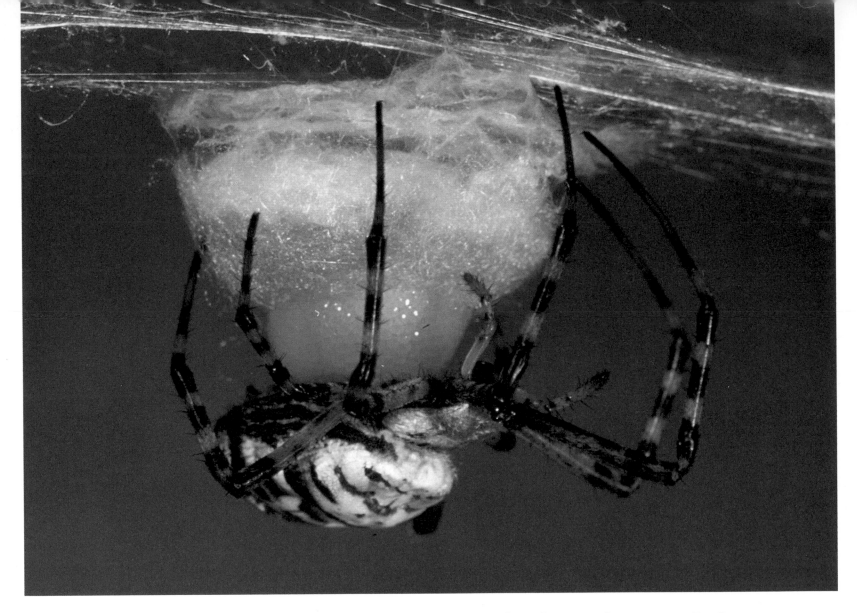

This female garden spider has mated and is laying her eggs. Before she started, she spun a sort of silk cradle. Her bright yellow eggs are coated with a sticky liquid. She gently pushes the mass of eggs into a ball. By the time she's done, she will have laid about 1,000 eggs. She lays so many eggs because not all of them will hatch. Many of her young will also be eaten by birds, insects, or other spiders.

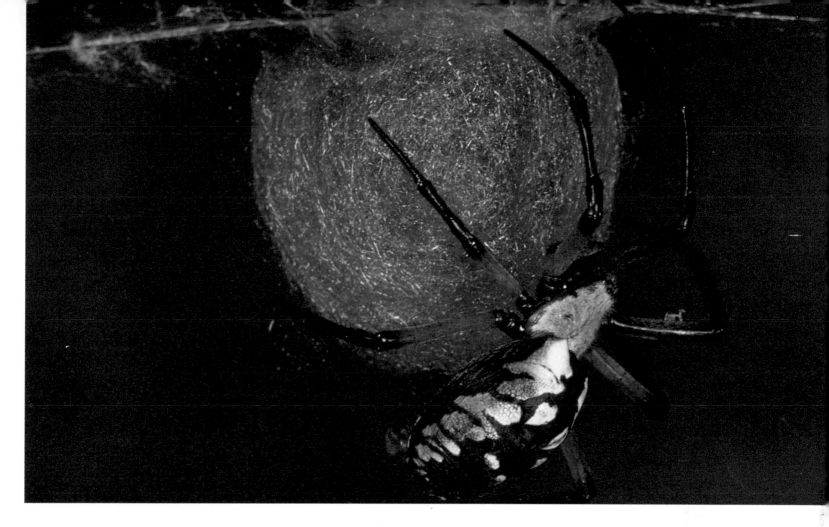

After she has finished laying her eggs, the female covers them with silk. Next, she adds more silk strands, which she draws out in loops with her hind legs. She pats these onto the egg sac. Finally, the female garden spider weaves a smooth covering of white silk. And she spins a few threads to attach the egg sac to nearby leaves or twigs.

The mother garden spider stays close to her egg sac for a few days, checking her work. If any of the strands holding the egg sac break, she repairs them. During this time, the covering of the egg sac becomes hard and turns brown.

Some female spiders go away and leave their egg sacs all alone. Others, like the female garden spider, lay their eggs in the fall and die a short time later. Still others keep a careful watch over their eggs. A female tarantula keeps her egg sac in her burrow. She guards it for about seven weeks, until the baby spiders hatch.

This female wolf spider has her egg sac stuck to her tail end by silk threads. It will take the baby spiders about three weeks to develop before they are ready to hatch. While the babies are growing, the female wolf spider carries her egg sac with her wherever she goes.

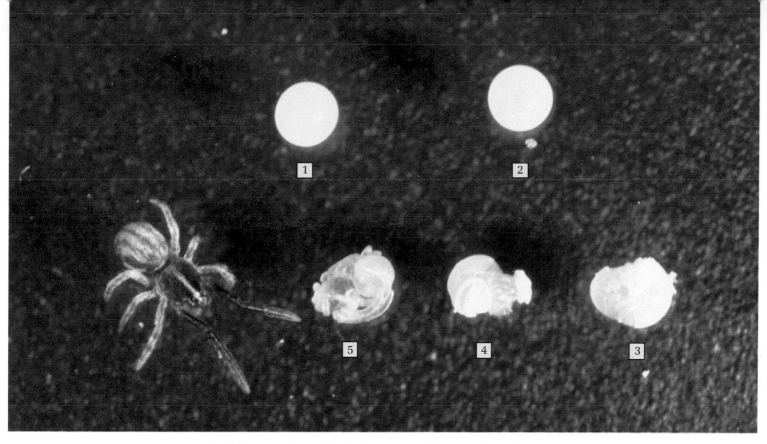

Find the egg where the baby spider's legs are first developed enough to show up clearly.

Now here's a surprise. You can peek through a spider egg's clear coat to see the baby spider growing inside.

Look at each of the numbered eggs in order to see how the young spider changes as it gets ready to hatch. Food for the baby spider growing inside the egg is supplied by a yolk. But a spider egg's yolk is not like the yolk of a chicken egg. It is tiny bits of food nutrients packed together.

The young spider's pedipalps have sharp edges called egg teeth. When the spider is ready to hatch, it uses these to tear open its egg. Then it crawls out.

31

These young garden spiders grew inside their eggs all winter. When spring arrived, they hatched. They will stay inside the egg sac just long enough to molt for the first time. Then they will chew their way out through the sac's silk walls.

Some mother spiders do take care of their young after they hatch. One type of funnel-web spider catches prey and brings it to her young. They live with her for about a month before going off on their own.

See all the spiderlings riding on this female wolf spider's back? The baby wolf spiders will stay with their mother for about a week. During this time, they will continue to live on what food was left from their yolk supply. When this food runs out, the spiders will drop off.

Then each little spider will go hunting. And all of its body parts will work together to let the young spider stay safe, find food, and grow. Clearly, spiders are special from the inside out.

This mother wolf spider bit open her egg sac to help her babies get out. Then they climbed aboard, holding onto her hairs to keep from falling off.

PRONUNCIATION GUIDE

ABDOMEN   ab´ də mən

ANTENNAE   an ten´ ē

CARBON DIOXIDE kär´ bən dī äk´ sīd

MOLTING   mōlt´ iŋ

NUTRIENT   nōō´ trē ənt

OXYGEN   äk´ si jən

PEDIPALP   ped´ i palp,

PREY   prā

SPIGOT   spig´ ət

TARANTULA   tə ran´ chōō lə

VENOM   ven´ əm

ə as in b**a**nan**a**   ä as in c**a**rt   ŋ as in si**ng**

GLOSSARY/INDEX

ABDOMEN: The back part of the spider's body which is separated from the combined head and chest section by a slim waist. **5, 24, 27**

ANTENNAE: Moveable jointed feelers on an insect's head which help it be aware of what's around it. Spiders never have antennae. **5**

BLACK WIDOW SPIDER: This spider is recognized by its black body with a red hourglass marking on the abdomen. **7, 10**

BOOK LUNGS: See **LUNGS**.

CARBON DIOXIDE: A gas that is given off as a waste when oxygen combines with food nutrients to produce energy. Blood carries it to the book lungs and sometimes through special tubes to openings in the spider's abdomen. There it passes into the air. **24**

COMB-FOOTED SPIDER: Type of spider found in people's houses whose webs are often called cobwebs. **6**

CRAB SPIDER: This spider got its name because it walks and runs like the familiar sea creature. These hunting spiders ambush their prey, hiding where their special coloring makes them hard to see. **14–15**

EGG SAC: The protective silk case surrounding the spider's eggs. **10, 28–30, 32, 33**

FANG: A sharp tooth used to inject a poisonous liquid called venom into the spider's prey. **15, 21**

FISHING SPIDER: With its front legs on the water, this spider detects the vibrations of small fish and dives underwater to catch its prey. **4–5**

FUNNEL-WEB SPIDER: True to its name, this spider builds a funnel-shaped web trap. **8, 10, 32**

GARDEN SPIDER: This spider's web trap is complete with sticky droplets to help keep prey from escaping. **8, 28–30, 32**

HEART: A tube-shaped muscle in spiders that pushes blood into smaller tubes. When these tubes end, the blood flows out, flooding the spider's body parts. **25**

JUMPING SPIDER: Its special eyes help the jumping spider find food, sense a mate, and be aware of an enemy in time to escape. **16–17, 18, 19, 26**

LARGE ORB-WEB WEAVER: Sticky droplets help make this spider's web an even better trap. **10, 20–22**

LUNGS: Body part where oxygen moves into the blood from the air and carbon dioxide seeps out of the spider's body into the air. They are called book lungs because they are made up of stacks of paper-thin, blood-filled layers. **24**

MOLTING: The process the spider goes through to shed its old body suit so it can be replaced by a new one. **13, 32**

NURSERY SPIDER: To encourage a female to mate, a male nursery spider carries along a food gift. **26**

NUTRIENTS: Chemical building blocks into which food is broken down for use by the spider's body. The five basic nutrients provided by foods are proteins, fats, carbohydrates, minerals, and vitamins. **23, 31**

OXYGEN: A gas in the air that seeps into the spider's lungs through slits in its abdomen. Blood carries the oxygen throughout the spider's body. Oxygen is combined with food nutrients to produce the energy the spider needs to live and grow. **24**

PEDIPALPS: Short leg-like parts close to a spider's mouth that help it catch and hold onto food. Males also use their pedipalps to transfer sperm to the female's body. **4, 5, 19, 27, 31**

PREY: The food the spider catches and eats. **15, 17, 21, 32**

RED-BACK SPIDER: A relative of the black widow commonly found in Australia and New Zealand. **27**

SILK: Special material produced by spiders to create a safety line and build a protective sac around their eggs. Some also use silk to make a web trap to catch food. Silk begins as a liquid, flows out through tiny tubes and spigots, and is pulled to make it change into a solid strand. **6–12, 17, 21, 28–29, 32**

SPIGOTS: Openings on the spider's tail end where silk shoots out. Different-shaped spigots are connected to different types of silk glands to make different kinds of silk. **6, 7**

STOMACH: This body part has large muscles to suck in the spider's liquid food. **22, 23**

TARANTULA: The biggest type of spider. **3, 15, 19, 24–25, 30**

TRAP-DOOR SPIDER: This spider uses its jaws to dig a burrow. It lines the burrow with silk and constructs a door complete with a silk hinge. This hinge lets the door stay almost shut while the spider hides, waiting to ambush its prey. The female lays her eggs inside the tunnel, and the young stay with her for a few weeks after hatching. **12**

VENOM: The liquid poison that flows into the prey when the spider bites. The venom may kill or only stun the prey. **15, 21**

WEB: A silk trap woven by some spiders. **6, 8–10, 21, 27**

WOLF SPIDER: This wandering hunter is noted for taking care of its young. The female first carries along its egg sac and then the young spiders. **10, 18, 30, 33**

YOLK: Bits of food nutrients packed together inside the egg that nourish the young spider while it's developing. **31, 33**

PHOTO CREDITS

Cover: courtesy Maria Zorn

Page 2: courtesy Texas Parks and Wildlife

Page 3: courtesy Leroy Williams

Page 4: courtesy Simon Pollard

Page 5: courtesy Texas Parks and Wildlife

Page 6: courtesy James Cokendolpher

Page 7: courtesy Bruce Cutler. 1,000 x

Page 8: courtesy Robert W. Parvin

Page 9: courtesy Simon Pollard

Page 10: courtesy Simon Pollard

Page 11: courtesy Simon Pollard

Page 12: courtesy Simon Pollard

Page 13: courtesy James Cokendolpher

Page 14: courtesy Simon Pollard

Page 15: courtesy James Cokendolpher

Page 16: courtesy Nic Bishop

Page 18: courtesy James Cokendolpher

Page 19: courtesy Bruce Cutler. 1,500 x [top]; 170 x [bottom]

Page 20: courtesy Simon Pollard

Page 21: courtesy Simon Pollard

Page 22: courtesy Simon Pollard

Page 23: courtesy Bruce Cutler. 250 x

Page 24: courtesy James Cokendolpher

Page 25: courtesy James Cokendolpher

Page 26: courtesy Simon Pollard

Page 27: courtesy Simon Pollard

Page 28: courtesy Maria Zorn

Page 29: courtesy Maria Zorn

Page 30: courtesy James Cokendolpher

Page 31: courtesy James Cokendolpher

Page 32: courtesy Maria Zorn

Page 33: courtesy Maria Zorn

Page 34: courtesy James Cokendolpher

LOOKING BACK

1. What kind of spider is the girl holding on page 3? Do you think she was brave to hold this spider? What do you think the spider felt like?

2. Spiders that build webs "feel" when something touches their webs. Why do you think the fishing spider on page 4 is touching the surface of the water? Look up fishing spider in the glossary.

3. Look at the web on page 8. Does it surprise you to learn that a spider only needs about 30 minutes to build a web? Most spiders even do their web-building in the dark, using their sense of touch to measure and space the threads. Get two pieces of yarn or string. Try arranging them in two evenly-spaced straight lines with your eyes closed. How well did you do?

4. Spiders eat their own silk. Do you remember why? If not, look back on pages 9 and 11.

5. Look at the spider next to its molted body suit on page 13. Imagine that you are a spider. How do you think it would feel to have to shed a body suit to grow bigger? Why would you want to hide while you are molting?

6. Look at the picture on page 14. Make up a story about what happened.

7. Look at the picture on page 16. Have you ever seen a picture of someone climbing a mountain or washing the windows outside a tall skyscraper? How do these people copy the spider?

8. Look at the pictures on page 19. Imagine that you could walk up the walls and stand upside down on the ceiling. How do you think your house and family would look from up there?

9. Look at the baby spiders on page 33. Why do you think the mother carries them on her back for about a week?

10. Look at the web on page 34. Do you think this spider chose a good place to spin its web? Why?